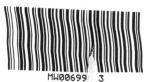

MW00699 3

BIBLE

christian
art gifts®

My Little Bible

© 1995 Christian Art Gifts, RSA
   Christian Art Gifts Inc., IL, USA

Second edition 2004
Third edition 2014

Designed by Christian Art Gifts
Compiled by Christian Art Gifts

Scripture taken from the *Holy Bible*, King James Ver
Copyright © 1962 by The Zondervan Corporation. Us
permission.

Printed in China

ISBN 978-1-86920-437-2 (Black)

16 17 18 19 20 21 22 23 24 25 - 13 12 11 10 9 8 7 6

Heaven and earth
shall pass away,
but my words
shall not pass away.

Matthew 24:35

My Little Bible presents
key Scripture verses
from every book
of the Bible.

May you be truly blessed
as you read from
God's precious Word.

Contents

Key Bible Sections

OLD TESTAMENT

GENESIS

In the beginning God created the heaven and the earth. *(1:1)*

God said, Let us make man in our image, after our likeness. *(1:26)*

God blessed the seventh day, and sanctified it: because that in it he had rested from all his work which God created and made. *(2:3)*

I will bless thee, and make thy name great; and thou shalt be a blessing ... and in thee shall all families of the earth be blessed. *(12:2-3)*

EXODUS

I will take you to me for a people, and I will be to you a God: and ye shall know that I am the LORD your God, which bringeth you out from under the burdens of the Egyptians. *(6:7)*

I am the LORD thy God, which have brought thee out of the land of Egypt, out of the house of bondage. Thou shalt have no other gods before me. *(20:2-3)*

The Ten Commandments

Thou shalt have no other gods before me.

Thou shalt not make unto thee any graven image.

Thou shalt not take the name of the LORD thy God in vain.

Remember the sabbath day, to keep it holy.

Honour thy father and thy mother.

Thou shalt not kill.

Thou shalt not commit adultery.

Thou shalt not steal.

Thou shalt not bear false witness against thy neighbour.

Thou shalt not covet. *(20:1-17)*

LEVITICUS

And this shall be an everlasting statute unto you, to make an atonement ... for all their sins once a year. *(16:34)*

And I will walk among you, and will be your God, and ye shall be my people. *(26:12)*

NUMBERS

The LORD bless thee, and keep thee: The LORD make his face shine upon thee, and be gracious unto thee: The LORD lift up his countenance upon thee, and give thee peace. *(6:24-26)*

DEUTERONOMY

Know therefore that the LORD thy God, he is God, the faithful God, which keepeth covenant and mercy with them that love him and keep his commandments. *(7:9)*

What doth the LORD thy God require of thee, but to fear the LORD thy God, to walk in all his ways, and to love him, and to serve the LORD thy God with all thy heart and with all thy soul. *(10:12)*

JOSHUA

This book of the law shall not depart out of thy mouth; but thou shalt meditate therein day and night, that thou mayest observe to do according to all that is written therein: for then thou shalt make thy way prosperous, and then thou shalt have good success. *(1:8)*

Be strong and of a good courage; be not afraid, neither be thou dismayed: for the LORD thy God is with thee whithersoever thou goest. *(1:9)*

And the LORD gave unto Israel all the land which he sware to give unto their fathers. The LORD delivered all their enemies into their hand. *(21:43-44)*

Fear the LORD, and serve him in sincerity and truth: and put away the gods which your forefathers served; and serve ye the LORD. *(24:14)*

Choose you this day whom ye will serve ... but as for me and my house, we will serve the LORD. *(24:15)*

JUDGES

Thus saith the LORD God of Israel, I brought you up from Egypt, and brought you forth out of the house of bondage. *(6:8)*

In those days there was no king in Israel: every man did that which was right in his own eyes. *(21:25)*

RUTH

And Ruth said, For whither thou goest, I will go; and where thou lodgest, I will lodge: thy people shall be my people, and thy God my God. *(1:16)*

1 SAMUEL

Hath the LORD as great delight in burnt offerings and sacrifices, as in obeying the voice of the LORD? Behold, to obey is better than sacrifice. *(15:22)*

For man looketh on the outward appearance, but the LORD looketh on the heart. *(16:7)*

2 SAMUEL

The LORD is my rock, and my fortress, and my deliverer; the God of my rock; in him will I trust. *(22:2-3)*

1 KINGS

If thou wilt walk before me ... in integrity of heart, and in uprightness ... and wilt keep my statutes and my judgments: Then I will establish the throne of thy kingdom upon Israel for ever. *(9:4-5)*

2 KINGS

O LORD God of Israel, which dwellest between the cherubims, thou art the God, even thou alone, of all the kingdoms of the earth; thou hast made heaven and earth. *(19:15)*

1 CHRONICLES

O give thanks unto the LORD; for he is good; for his mercy endureth for ever. Save us, O God of our salvation, and deliver us, that we may give thanks to thy holy name. *(16:34-35)*

2 CHRONICLES

If my people, which are called by my name, shall humble themselves, and pray, and seek my face, and turn from their wicked ways; then will I hear from heaven, and will forgive their sin, and will heal their land. *(7:14)*

EZRA

For the LORD had made them joyful, and turned the heart of the king of Assyria unto them, to strengthen their hands in the work of the house of God, the God of Israel. *(6:22)*

NEHEMIAH

So the wall was finished. And it came to pass that when all our enemies heard thereof and saw these things, they perceived that this work was wrought of our God. *(6:15-16)*

Esther

Who knoweth whether thou art come to the kingdom for such a time as this? *(4:14)*

Job

Though he may slay me, yet will I trust in him: I will maintain mine own ways before him. He also shall be my salvation. *(13:15-16)*

But he knoweth the way that I take: when he hath tried me, I shall come forth as gold. *(23:10)*

Psalms

The heavens declare the glory of God; and the firmament sheweth his handywork. *(19:1)*

Give unto the LORD the glory due unto his name; worship the LORD in the beauty of holiness. *(29:2)*

O come, let us sing unto the LORD: let us make a joyful noise to the rock of our salvation. *(95:1)*

Know ye that the LORD he is God: we are his people, and the sheep of his pasture. *(100:3)*

Blessed are the undefiled in the way, who walk in the law of the LORD. Blessed are they that keep his testimonies, and that seek him with the whole heart. *(119:1-2)*

I will lift up mine eyes unto the hills, from whence cometh my help. My help cometh from the LORD, which made heaven and earth. *(121:1-2)*

Let every thing that hath breath praise the LORD. Praise ye the LORD. *(150:6)*

Psalm 23

The LORD is my shepherd; I shall not want.

He maketh me to lie down in green pastures: he leadeth me beside the still waters.

He restoreth my soul: he leadeth me in the paths of righteousness for his name's sake.

Yea, though I walk through the valley of the shadow of death, I will fear no evil: for thou art with me; thy rod and thy staff they comfort me.

Thou preparest a table before me in the presence of mine enemies: thou anointest my head with oil; my cup runneth over.

Surely goodness and mercy shall follow me all the days of my life: and I will dwell in the house of the LORD for ever.

PROVERBS

Trust in the LORD with all thine heart; and lean not unto thine own understanding. In all thy ways acknowledge him, and he shall direct thy paths. *(3:5-6)*

The fear of the LORD is the beginning of wisdom: and the knowledge of the holy is understanding. *(9:10)*

A good name is rather to be chosen than great riches, and loving favour rather than silver and gold. *(22:1)*

ECCLESIASTES

To every thing there is a season, and a time to every purpose under the heaven. *(3:1)*

Let us hear the conclusion of the whole matter: Fear God, and keep his commandments: for this is the whole duty of man. *(12:13)*

SONG OF SOLOMON

He brought me to the banqueting house, and his banner over me was love. *(2:4)*

ISAIAH

Come now, and let us reason together, saith the LORD: though your sins be as scarlet, they shall be as white as snow. *(1:18)*

Therefore the Lord himself shall give you a sign; Behold, a virgin shall conceive, and bear a son, and shall call his name Immanuel. *(7:14)*

But he was wounded for our transgressions, he was bruised for our iniquities: the chastisement of our peace was upon him; and with his stripes we are healed. *(53:5)*

JEREMIAH

For I know the thoughts that I think toward you, saith the LORD, thoughts of peace, and not of evil, to give you an expected end. *(29:11)*

Behold, I am the LORD, the God of all flesh: is there any thing too hard for me? *(32:27)*

I will cleanse them from all their iniquity, whereby they have sinned against me; and I will pardon all their iniquities, whereby they have sinned, and whereby they have transgressed against me. *(33:8)*

LAMENTATIONS

His compassions fail not. They are new every morning: great is thy faithfulness. *(3:22-23)*

Let us search and try our ways, and turn again to the LORD. *(3:40)*

EZEKIEL

A new heart also will I give you, and a new spirit will I put within you ... and cause you to walk in my statutes, and ye shall keep my judgments, and do them. *(36:26-27)*

DANIEL

He changeth the times and the seasons ... he giveth wisdom unto the wise, and knowledge to them that know understanding. He revealeth the deep and secret things: he knoweth what is in the darkness. *(2:21-22)*

If it be so, our God whom we serve is able to deliver us from the burning fiery furnace, and he will deliver us out of thine hand, O king. But if not, be it known unto thee, O king, that we will not serve thy gods. *(3:17-18)*

And there was given him dominion, and glory, and a kingdom,
that all people, nations, and lan-
guages, should serve him ... and
his kingdom ... shall not be de-
stroyed. *(7:14)*

HOSEA
I will betroth thee unto me for
ever; yea, I will betroth thee unto
me in righteousness, and in judg-
ment, and in lovingkindness, and
in mercies. I will even betroth thee
unto me in faithfulness: and thou
shalt know the LORD. *(2:19-20)*

I will have mercy upon her that had not obtained mercy; and I will say to them which were not my people, Thou art my people; and they shall say, Thou art my God. *(2:23)*

JOEL

Turn unto the LORD your God: for he is gracious and merciful, slow to anger, and of great kindness. *(2:13)*

AMOS

Seek good, and not evil, that ye may live: and so the LORD ... shall be with you. *(5:14)*

OBADIAH
As thou hast done, it shall be done unto thee: thy reward shall return upon thine own head. *(1:15)*

JONAH
When my soul fainted within me I remembered the LORD: and my prayer came in unto thee, into thine holy temple. *(2:7)*

MICAH
What doth the LORD require of thee, but to do justly, and to love mercy, and to walk humbly with thy God? *(6:8)*

NAHUM

The LORD is good, a strong hold in the day of trouble; and he knoweth them that trust in him. *(1:7)*

HABAKKUK

O LORD, revive thy work in the midst of the years, in the midst of the years make known; in wrath remember mercy. *(3:2)*

ZEPHANIAH

The LORD thy God in the midst of thee is mighty; he will save, he will rejoice over thee with joy; he will rest in his love, he will joy over thee with singing. *(3:17)*

HAGGAI

The glory of this latter house shall be greater than of the former, saith the LORD of hosts: and in this place will I give peace, saith the LORD of hosts. *(2:9)*

ZECHARIAH

Turn ye unto me, saith the LORD of hosts, and I will turn unto you, saith the LORD of hosts. *(1:3)*

MALACHI

Unto you that fear my name shall the Sun of righteousness arise with healing in his wings; and ye shall go forth. *(4:2)*

New Testament

MATTHEW

Thou shalt call his name JESUS: for he shall save his people from their sins. *(1:21)*

Seek ye first the kingdom of God, and his righteousness; and all these things shall be added unto you. *(6:33)*

Come unto me, all ye that labour and are heavy laden, and I will give you rest. *(11:28)*

Whosoever will save his life shall lose it: and whosoever will lose his life for my sake shall find it. For what is a man profited, if he shall gain the whole world, and lose his own soul? *(16:25-26)*

Set up over his head his accusation written, THIS IS JESUS THE KING OF THE JEWS. *(27:37)*

The angel answered and said unto the women, Fear not ye: for I know that ye seek Jesus, which was crucified. He is not here: for he is risen, as he said. Come, see the place where the Lord lay. (28:5-6)

The Lord's Prayer

Our Father which art in heaven, Hallowed be thy name.

Thy kingdom come, Thy will be done in earth, as it is in heaven.

Give us this day our daily bread.

And forgive us our debts, as we forgive our debtors.

And lead us not into temptation, but deliver us from evil: For thine is the kingdom, and the power, and the glory, for ever. Amen. *(6:9-13)*

The Great Commission

Jesus came and spake unto them, saying, All power is given unto me in heaven and in earth.

Go ye therefore, and teach all nations, baptizing them in the name of the Father, and of the Son, and of the Holy Ghost:

Teaching them to observe all things whatsoever I have commanded you: and, lo, I am with you always, even unto the end of the world. Amen. *(28:18-20)*

MARK

Suffer the little children to come unto me, and forbid them not: for of such is the kingdom of God. *(10:14)*

For even the Son of man came not to be ministered unto, but to minister, and to give his life a ransom for many. *(10:45)*

LUKE

Blessed are they that hear the word of God, and keep it. *(11:28)*

For the Son of man is come to seek and to save that which was lost. *(19:10)*

JOHN

Verily, verily, I say unto thee, Except a man be born of water and of the Spirit, he cannot enter into the kingdom of God. *(3:5)*

For God so loved the world, that he gave his only begotten Son, that whosoever believeth in him should not perish, but have everlasting life. *(3:16)*

I am the way, the truth, and the life: no man cometh unto the Father, but by me. *(14:6)*

ACTS

Ye shall receive power, after that the Holy Ghost is come upon you: and ye shall be witnesses unto me both in Jerusalem, and in all Judaea, and in Samaria, and unto the uttermost part of the earth. *(1:8)*

They continued stedfastly in the apostles' doctrine and fellowship, and in breaking of bread, and in prayers. *(2:42)*

Believe on the Lord Jesus Christ, and thou shalt be saved. *(16:31)*

ROMANS

I am not ashamed of the gospel of Christ: for it is the power of God unto salvation to every one that believeth. *(1:16)*

All have sinned, and come short of the glory of God. *(3:23)*

The wages of sin is death; but the gift of God is eternal life through Jesus Christ our Lord. *(6:23)*

We know that all things work together for good to them that love God, to them who are the called according to his purpose. *(8:28)*

1 CORINTHIANS

Eye hath not seen, nor ear heard, neither have entered into the heart of man, the things which God hath prepared for them that love him. *(2:9)*

Know ye not that your body is the temple of the Holy Ghost ... For ye are bought with a price: therefore glorify God in your body, and in your spirit, which are God's. *(6:19-20)*

Now abideth faith, hope, charity; but the greatest of these is charity. *(13:13)*

2 CORINTHIANS

If any man be in Christ, he is a new creature: old things are passed away; behold, all things are become new. *(5:17)*

My grace is sufficient for thee: for my strength is made perfect in weakness. Most gladly therefore will I rather glory in my infirmities, that the power of Christ may rest upon me. *(12:9)*

Be of one mind, live in peace; and the God of love and peace shall be with you. *(13:11)*

GALATIANS

A man is not justified by the works of the law, but by the faith of Jesus Christ. *(2:16)*

I am crucified with Christ: nevertheless I live; yet not I, but Christ liveth in me: and the life which I now live in the flesh I live by the faith of the Son of God, who loved me, and gave himself for me. *(2:20)*

The fruit of the Spirit is love, joy, peace, longsuffering, gentleness, goodness, faith, meekness, temperance: against such there is no law. *(5:22-23)*

EPHESIANS

Blessed be the God and Father of our Lord Jesus Christ, who hath blessed us with all spiritual blessings in heavenly places in Christ. *(1:3)*

For by grace are ye saved through faith; and that not of yourselves: it is the gift of God. For we are his workmanship, created in Christ Jesus unto good works, which God hath before ordained that we should walk in them. *(2:8, 10)*

PHILIPPIANS

For to me to live is Christ, and to die is gain. *(1:21)*

Rejoice in the Lord always: and again I say, Rejoice. *(4:4)*

COLOSSIANS

In him dwelleth all the fulness of the Godhead bodily. And ye are complete in him. *(2:9-10)*

Set your affection on things above, not on things on the earth. *(3:2)*

1 Thessalonians

The Lord himself shall descend from heaven with a shout ... and the dead in Christ shall rise first: Then we which are alive ... shall be caught up together with them in the clouds, to meet the Lord in the air. *(4:16-17)*

Rejoice evermore. Pray without ceasing. In every thing give thanks. *(5:16-18)*

2 Thessalonians

The Lord direct your hearts into the love of God, and into the patient waiting for Christ. *(3:5)*

1 TIMOTHY

Let no man despise thy youth; but be thou an example of the believers, in word, in conversation, in charity, in spirit, in faith, in purity. *(4:12)*

2 TIMOTHY

Grace, mercy and peace, from God the Father and Christ Jesus our Lord. *(1:2)*

Study to shew thyself approved unto God, a workman that needeth not to be ashamed, rightly dividing the word of truth. *(2:15)*

TITUS

Not by works of righteousness which we have done, but according to his mercy he saved us, by the washing of regeneration, and renewing of the Holy Ghost. *(3:5)*

PHILEMON

I thank my God, making mention of thee always in my prayers. *(1:4)*

A brother beloved, specially to me ... both in the flesh, and in the Lord. *(1:16)*

HEBREWS

Now faith is the substance of things hoped for, the evidence of things not seen. *(11:1)*

Without faith it is impossible to please him: for he that cometh to God must believe that he is, and that he is a rewarder of them that diligently seek him. *(11:6)*

For he hath said, I will never leave thee, nor forsake thee. So that we may boldly say, The Lord is my helper, and I will not fear what man shall do unto me. *(13:5-6)*

JAMES

Be ye doers of the word, and not hearers only, deceiving your own selves. *(1:22)*

Submit yourselves therefore to God. Resist the devil, and he will flee from you. *(4:7)*

To him that knoweth to do good, and doeth it not, to him it is sin. *(4:17)*

The effectual fervent prayer of a righteous man availeth much. *(5:16)*

1 Peter

Your faith, being much more precious than of gold that perisheth, though it be tried with fire, might be found unto praise and honour and glory at the appearing of Jesus Christ. *(1:7)*

For even hereunto were ye called: because Christ also suffered for us, leaving us an example, that ye should follow his steps. *(2:21)*

2 Peter

His divine power hath given unto us all things that pertain unto life and godliness. *(1:3)*

1 JOHN

If we confess our sins, he is faithful and just to forgive us our sins, and to cleanse us from all unrighteousness. *(1:9)*

These things have I written unto you that believe on the name of the Son of God; that ye may know that ye have eternal life. *(5:13)*

2 JOHN

This is love, that we walk after his commandments. *(1:6)*

3 JOHN

I have no greater joy than to hear that my children walk in truth. *(1:4)*

JUDE

But ye, beloved, building up yourselves on your most holy faith, praying in the Holy Ghost, keep yourselves in the love of God, looking for the mercy of our Lord Jesus Christ unto eternal life. *(20-21)*

Now unto him that is able to keep you from falling, and to present you faultless before the presence of his glory with exceeding joy, to the only wise God our Saviour, be glory and majesty, dominion and power, both now and ever. Amen. *(24-25)*

REVELATION

Fear not; I am the first and the last: I am he that liveth, and was dead; and, behold, I am alive for evermore, Amen. *(1:17-18)*

He that hath an ear, let him hear what the Spirit saith unto the churches; to him that overcometh will I give to eat of the tree of life, which is in the midst of the paradise of God. *(2:7)*

Behold, I stand at the door, and knock: if any man hear my voice, and open the door, I will come in. *(3:20)*

Where to find it in the Scriptures

Anxiety and worry – Phil. 4; Ps. 37; 1 Pet. 5

Assurance – John 14; Rom. 8; 1 John 5

Beatitudes – Matt. 5

Courage – Josh. 1

Comfort – 2 Cor. 1

Devil – Gen. 3; Isa. 14; Matt. 4; Rev. 12

Death – 1 Cor. 15; 1 Thess. 4; Rev. 21-22; Ps. 23

Depression – Ps. 34, 42-43

Education – Deut. 6

Faith – Heb. 11

Family – Eph. 5-6

Fear – Ps. 121

Forgiveness of sin – Ps. 51; Acts 2; 1 John 1

Fruitful life in Christ – John 15

Prayer — Matt. 6; Mark 11; Eph. 3

Physical illness — Ps. 6, 39, 41

Problems come your way — Heb. 12

Quick tongue — James 2

Ressurection — 1 Cor. 15

Sin — Ps. 51; Rom. 3

Salvation — Acts 2, 9, 16; Rom. 5-6

Spirit-filled life — Rom. 8

Suffering trials — 2 Cor. 1; James 1

Temptation — 1 Cor. 10

Unity — Eph. 4; Col. 2; John 17; Rom. 12

Victory — Rom. 6-8

Word of God — Ps. 119; Heb. 4

Wisdom — Prov. 3; 1 Cor. 2

Youth — Eccles. 12; 2 Tim. 2

Who am I in Christ?

CHOSEN BY GOD:

He hath chosen us in him before the foundation of the world, that we should be holy and without blame (Eph. 1:4).

MADE PERFECT FOREVER:

For by one offering he hath perfected for ever them that are sanctified (Heb. 10:14).

REDEEMED:

In whom we have redemption through his blood, the forgiveness of sins (Eph. 1:7).

MADE AT PEACE WITH GOD:

Therefore being justified by faith, we have peace with God through our Lord Jesus Christ (Rom. 5:1).

Totally forgiven:

And you, being dead in your sins ... hath he quickened together with him, having forgiven you all trespasses (Col. 2:13).

Totally cleansed:

Ye are washed, but ye are sanctified, but ye are justified in the name of the Lord Jesus, and by the Spirit of our God (1 Cor. 6:11).

Made holy and blameless:

In the body of his flesh through death, to present you holy and unblameable and unreproveable in his sight (Col. 1:22).

Given Christ's righteousness:

He hath made him to be sin for us, who knew no sin; that we might be made the righteousness of God in him (2 Cor. 5:21).

FREED FROM CONDEMNATION:

There is therefore now no condemnation to them which are in Christ Jesus, who walk not after the flesh, but after the Spirit (Rom. 8:1).

MADE INTO A NEW CREATION:

Therefore if any man be in Christ, he is a new creature: old things are passed away; behold, all things are become new (2 Cor. 5:17).

RECONCILED TO GOD:

We were reconciled to God by the death of his Son, much more, being reconciled, we shall be saved by his life (Rom. 5:10).

MADE HEIRS OF GOD:

Wherefore thou art no more a servant, but a son; and if a son, then an heir of God through Christ (Gal. 4:7).

My Little Bible
TB008

ISBN 978-1-86920-437-2

9 781869 204372